DRIED FLOWERS
FOR WINTER
ARRANGEMENTS

DRIED FLOWERS FOR WINTER ARRANGEMENTS

Harold Piercy NDH DIP ED (BIRMINGHAM)
Principal of the
Constance Spry Flower School

BRITISH HERITAGE AND JONATHAN CAPE
THIRTY BEDFORD SQUARE LONDON WCI

© 1971 Constance Spry Ltd
© 1971 Jonathan Cape Ltd and Heritage Publishers Ltd
Printed in the Netherlands by N.V. Grafische Industrie Haarlem
ISBN 0 224 00574.X

Introduction

An intriguing aspect of flower arrangement is not only its popularity as a pastime and a commercial activity but also the extent to which growers, wholesalers of flowers and of seeds, journalists and publishers have been influenced by its surprisingly wide development.

In the nineteen-thirties comparatively few people, other than Constance Spry, were actively concerned in flower decoration in this country. Artistic or even interesting flower arrangement was an unexpected form of expression of taste and was remarkable, if noticed at all. Early in that decade, when she had just begun to make flowers her main occupation, Constance Spry wrote *Flower Decoration* (published by J. M. Dent & Sons), the first of a series of fascinating books, and the point of it came home to a wide public. Her flair was for simplicity in the use of flowers and for introducing unusual ones – unusual in the sense that many of them were not generally thought to be particularly beautiful or decorative or quite fashionable at that time. By 'doing the flowers' in such a way as to emphasise the most attractive characteristics of almost any room or background, she somehow lightened the place with a touch of magic, and set a style which remains outstanding today.

The influence of aspirants in this field grew and created a demand that had not existed before in markets or among other producers in the horticultural business; consequently the variety of things to be had became wider. Now, many plants and flowers, vases and accessories, once considered unusual, are no longer so, and this to a great extent is due to the enthusiastic activity of flower decorators. The idea, for instance of producing a seed-pack and guide, put together specially with arrangers in mind, is not new; it was thought of even in the early days referred to already, but there could hardly have been the impulse then to set such an undertaking off on the right foot. The pack introduced here is the outcome of a conjunction of timely ideas. Messrs Suttons, British Heritage and Mr Harold Piercy put their heads together and have ingeniously catered for a pressing demand by producing an appropriate seed collection as well as instructions to accompany it. To have a supply of garden produce for winter arrangements is no novelty. Goodness knows, a stiffly ornamental array of pampas grass in cylindrical pots, as a form of decoration, is old-fashioned enough, and nonetheless an amusing one to have, but the use of many different kinds of 'drieds' has come to be popular as the result of recent experiments with likely things to brighten the dead season of the year. Mr Piercy, a practical gardener as well as a teacher, has provided a guide not just to growing but to the rather more delicate processes involved in preserving flowers for winter decorations, and then to the ways of arranging them. He trained at Constance Spry's Flower School and now heads it as Principal; all the information he knows so well how to impart is given here with the generosity of an expert, and he puts before the reader another intriguing aspect of flower arrangement.

ANTHONY MARR

Winter flowers and foliage

When autumn comes and the garden is getting bare there is a lot to be said for brightening up the house with flowers that have been preserved. One can of course use plastic or other artificial flowers; but how much more pleasant are real ones that still retain some of the life and movement they had when fresh. And nowadays there is such a wealth of material available that really we have no excuse for not making use of it.

This book is about growing such materials, treating then to preserve them and finally arranging them. Some are preserved for their shape, others for their colour: but all with the purpose of extending their life for decoration in one form or another – whether in a conventional vase, a picture frame, or even under a Victorian glass dome (especially valuable because it keeps the arrangement clean and dry).

There are really two groups of dried materials. First we have bright-coloured flowers, dried in their prime to create winter colour and, as it were, carry summer over into winter. Secondly there are foliages and seed heads, dried or chemically treated to give more sombre brown-green arrangements. This second group is also valuable for its forms and textures – what could be more attractive in the winter months than a few shapely branches of beech to which a few 'shadow' leaves have been carefully attached? (For special occasions one can add to these four or five coffee-coloured rayonnante chrysanthemums.)

As a rule, I believe in using dried arrangements from the onset of autumn, when they tend to blend best with outside colourings, until the Christmas decorations go up. (After these have gone it is time to be looking for the first flowers of spring.) In any case they should not be allowed to remain once they have become over-dry, brittle and covered with dust. You can, of course, combine dried with living materials. Dried stems can stand for a while in a vase containing water, though as a safeguard against deterioration it is as well to treat them with a varnish or waterproofing paint: alternatively you can arrange them on their own in a flower tube which is placed in the vase of living materials.

Finally, remember that you can always keep any dried materials that remain in good order by cleaning them and storing them for another year in plastic bags. To stop them going damp in storage add a little drying agent such as silica gel (of which more later).

Sowing out of doors

Most flowers suitable for drying can also be used to give colour to your garden during the summer and so do double duty. The best idea is probably to grow some like this, in your flower borders, and some in nursery rows, out of sight, for cutting and drying in the latter part of the season.

The main demand of all of them is for open, sunny ground. It is seldom that you can choose your soil; but the ideal is a fairly open one, light in texture but with enough organic matter to retain moisture. Soil too rich in plant food will produce excessive leaf growth at the expense of flowers, which will be very late developing. On the other hand soil poor in food will bring about stunted growth and too early flowering – such flowers will be small and often rather highly coloured.

Prepare the ground in late autumn and during the winter with a view to sowing through the spring. Dig the soil over, removing any weeds, old roots and large stones; then leave it rough for frost action to break it down. If the soil is acid add a little lime after digging. Do not attempt to work the soil if it is at all sticky. Prior to sowing, firm it by gently treading and raking.

If you are growing your plants in nursery rows for

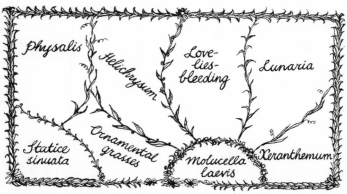

Possible border plan for flowers intended for drying

Sow thinly and evenly

cutting, set them far enough apart to enable you to use any mechanical equipment you may have. If your equipment consists of just an ordinary hoe, it is usual to set the plants at intervals of 9–12 in. in rows 15–18 in. apart.

If on the other hand you are growing them in a flower border just fit the plants into the existing pattern. In this case it is probably easier to raise the seeds somewhere else in the garden and plant them out when they are ready. Most plants, though not for instance xeranthemum, can be treated in this way.

Sow the seed thinly and evenly. There should be no competition for room such as occurs when seedlings are sown too thickly and cannot be thinned out at the appropriate time. Thinning can be done by chopping out with a small hoe or, if the ground is really moist, pulling the seedlings carefully like spring onions.

Thinning, watering, feeding and weeding are the only forms of attention your plants should need regularly. (It is important that the plants be kept free from pests and disease so that they are perfect when cut for drying. They always deteriorate slightly in the course of preservation, so they must be perfect when picked and treated as quickly as possible after cutting.) Hoe regularly to keep the soil open, and top dress with a dusting of plant food during the latter part of the growing season. Staking is necessary only for tall plants like helichrysum. If others do threaten to fall over, a little brushwood tucked in among the growing shoots will help to support them; but do this before it is absolutely necessary because once a plant has fallen over it never comes up quite straight again.

Plants should be grown quickly and without any checks to get the best results. Setbacks occasioned by choking weeds or bad weather will show up later on in the flowering season. (Plants for drying are always better in a dry summer.)

As soon as the flowers are fully developed, cut them carefully. Often, by taking out the main stem, you will induce side shoots to flower; and in a good long summer a second crop of flowers may be harvested from plants started early in the season.

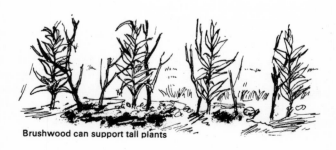
Brushwood can support tall plants

Sowing
in boxes

Sowing in boxes is quite a simple process if the following points are observed.

First it is essential to have a high quality compost of good texture, providing an adequate and balanced supply of food, and free from all harmful organisms. There are many composts made, but probably the most suitable is the John Innes Seed Compost. This is made up of good loam, moist peat and sharp sand: it retains moisture yet remains open in texture. Both chalk and plant food are added to allow maximum plant growth.

The compost should be freshly made, so it should be obtained from nursery sundriesmen when required. The seed compost is ideal for seed sowing and the first stages of plant development up to potting in $3\frac{1}{2}$-in. pots. Richer mixtures, such as John Innes Potting Compost No. 1, should be used for larger pots and growing on the more vigorous plants. This is made of the same ingredients in different proportions and contains more plant food.

To grow, seeds must be provided with moisture, warmth and air. The art of sowing seeds in boxes is to provide these conditions so that all the viable seeds will start to grow as soon as possible and make good plants.

A seed box of $2\frac{1}{2}$-in. depth, preferably made of wood,

Sow in wooden boxes or plastic trays

with good drainage gaps, is best, but some plastic seed trays are quite useful.

There is no need to place broken crock in the box if a good open compost is used. Seed beds of a greater depth than 2 in. remain cold and wet: the seedlings are not so easy to lift out from the seed bed, and waterlogged soil does not contain enough air for good growth. Seed beds under 2 in. in depth dry out too quickly. The condition of the compost should be such that when squeezed in the hand it retains its shape but crumbles down when tossed lightly from hand to hand. If too wet it is sticky to the touch, and when too dry it will not form to any mould.

Levelling the compost

Place the box on a flat bench against the heap of compost, draw two to three good handfuls into the box, level and lightly firm the corners and along the box edge. Then completely fill the seed box, scraping off the surplus compost with a straight edge. Tap each side of the box sharply on the bench three times – this will settle the bottom level of the compost.

Firm the top level of the compost with a 'presser' – ideally a piece of wood half the size of the box which has in its sides pegs set $\frac{1}{2}$ in. from the base to stop the presser going down too far. This will give an even, level seed bed which is firm but springy to the touch.

The seed should be sown evenly on this surface – allow equal space for each seed to give ideal growing conditions. If sown too deep it will take longer to germinate; if not sown deep enough the seedlings will fall over after germination or not grow properly.

For large seeds spot-sowing at regular intervals across the box will give the best results. Cover the seed with a thin layer of compost passed through a fine riddle ($\frac{1}{8}$ grist) giving approximately $\frac{1}{8}$ in. of cover soil over the whole box.

Spot sowing

Cover with glass
and newspaper after moistening

After covering do not firm. Stand the box in a shallow tray of water – about 1 in. deep – for a few minutes to allow the soil to become moist, then drain and place in the greenhouse or frame covered with a sheet of glass and then with a sheet of newspaper.

The paper should be removed as soon as the first seedlings show. The glass comes off shortly afterwards and before any seedlings touch it.

Sowing in pans, pots and half pans can be done in the same way. Two in. of soil is all that is necessary, the bottom of the container being filled with crock.

As soon as the seedlings are large enough to handle they should be pricked out into boxes of the same horizontal dimensions but 3 in. deep. John Innes No. 1 can be used. Handle the seedlings with great care – lift from the soil by holding the seed leaf and not the stem, after carefully loosening from the seed bed with a label.

Mark out the new seed box carefully, allowing equal space for each seedling: usually nine rows of six to a standard seed box 14 in. by 9 in. Make a hole with a blunt stick of pencil thickness and carefully place the young seedling in the hole, pressing slightly at the side of the stem with the stick to firm. (If you are using standard-size boxes a presser can be made to fit the box which has studs in its base – these will mark the soil sur-

Pricking out

face, and at each mark you can prick out a seedling.) If seedlings are of different sizes, try to grade them by boxes so that even growth will develop. After pricking out, water in carefully and replace in the greenhouse or frame.

Keep up to the light – do not allow plants to become drawn. At this stage pot up a few plants for house decoration. Grow on the others steadily, gradually hardening off, and plant outside in your border or cutting bed as soon as conditions are suitable – i.e. above all when frost is unlikely. It is important that the plants should not be checked at any time. Pot on those plants wanted as pot plants into large 60 and 48 pots. John Innes No. 2 can be used for final potting.

These pot plants can also be used for growing on in tubs, window boxes and plant stands both inside and outside the house. By using large pots one gets a quicker show and can maintain better continuity in window boxes.

Presser

Materials for dried arrangements

A wealth of materials is available nowadays to anyone wanting to make dried arrangements. For example, these are the main garden-grown flowers used in the arrangements illustrated at the end of the book:

Helichrysum (straw flower). There are annuals, perennials and woody shrubs in this genus; but it is only the annual *H. bracteatum* that is interesting for drying. It is normally grown for cutting in nursery rows where the necessary support can be given to ensure upright growth, but it can also go at the back of the annual border or anywhere else that is sunny and well drained. For drying, cut before the flowers are fully open and hang them upside down.

Ornamental grasses. These come in a wide variety of shapes and styles and are most valuable either on their own or to give a light effect to a flower arrangement, both in vases and in flower pictures. They are normally grown in nursery rows for cutting, not in the flower border. With them you can use any wild grasses and heads of corn such as oats, wheat, barley and water grass gathered in the country in early autumn. Pampas (*Cortaderia argentea*) is a particularly good form of large grass.

Xeranthemum. This is a popular flower for drying

with its soft colours and straw-textured flowers, and it is also useful for summer decorations when fresh. The flowers should be cut when just fully open and dried by hanging upside down in a cool, airy shed.

Statice sinuata. This attractive flower is effective in the border and can be used for arranging fresh or dry: in the latter form it is very long lasting. Frequently available in flower shops in August or September, it needs arranging carefully for best results: often part of the stem needs thinning out so that you get some well shaped pieces to arrange. Other forms of statice are worth growing. The perennial *Limonium latifolium* (sea lavender) is attractive arranged on its own in wall vases and hanging baskets. *Statice suworowi* has long, arching sprays of lilac-pink flowers like long cat's tails.

Moluccella (bells of Ireland). A member of the stinging nettle family, moluccella was once treated as a rare novelty for the arranger, but with the introduction of better seeds anyone can now raise it with a little care. It can be arranged with other drieds or on its own with just a few branches on to which 'shadow' leaves (skeletonized magnolia leaves) have been wired. It takes glycerine very well for preserving and can also be bleached by drying in heat.

Lunaria biennis (honesty). This hardy biennial is normally grown for the silvery moon-shaped membranes between the seed pods. However the whole seed pods can also be used: their grey-greenish colour suits some arrangements better than the natural silver of the centre membrane. The stems must be dried as soon as they are ready: if left too long the seed stains the silver membrane.

Love-lies-bleeding. In both fresh and dried form this is a most useful plant. Hang upside down to dry, being careful not to let the tassels become tangled. Its colours may fade, but it is still useful.

Physalis (Chinese lantern). The interest of this hardy perennial lies not in its flowers but in the pretty orange-scarlet seed vessels which remain at the end of the season and give it its popular name of Chinese lantern. (It is also called Cape gooseberry.) Dry by hanging upside down in small bunches, removing the foliage as it dies off; then store in a dry place with a little silica gel.

In addition to the wild grasses already mentioned, a walk along any country lane can provide you with many more materials. Among the most valuable are the sturdy umbrella-shaped plants such as wild **parsnip** and **fennel** and trails of wild **clematis** and **hops**. Wild **teazle** seed heads are excellent, and so are **iris** seed pods (the seeds must be lightly painted with gum arabic to secure them). Suitable for larger groups are **bulrushes**, which must be collected early and lightly sprayed with lacquer to stop them splitting when ripe and shedding their seed everywhere. Wild clematis and branches of **pussy willow** should be air dried.

Finally, here are some other garden plants worth growing for drying and using to add a touch of interest to an arrangement, as some of them do in the illustrations to this book:

Acanthus mollis. The leaves are excellent in fresh-flower decoration, and the flower spikes when dried have an interesting shape for working into large groups. They dry easily when hung upside down in an airy shed.

Acroclinium. The gaily coloured daisy-form flowers of this hardy annual are equally suitable for garden decoration and for subsequent drying. Flower heads can sometimes be bought ready dried and are effective, for example, affixed to plaques.

Catananche coerulea (Cupid's dart). This flower's particular advantages are its bright blue blooms, larger than most of the daisy types, and its long, silver-grey stems. There are also annual forms of this hardy perennial: a popular one is *Catananche lutea*, which is shorter than *C. coerulea* and has yellow flowers.

Rhodanthe. Like many of the Australian everlastings, this pretty flower has straw-textured petals and is attractive both in the garden and dried. It can also be grown in pots for indoor decoration or in tubs and window boxes. It looks well when arranged with silver-grey foliage.

Allium. This is the genus that comprises onions, chives, leeks etc. The long, slender stems are effective cut after flowering and hung upside down to dry. One slight disadvantage is the faint smell that always remains.

Atriplex hortensis. This hardy annual is a member of the spinach family with dark red leaves. It is useful in summer and autumn in cut flower arrangements, and in winter, after careful drying, it gives arching branches of pendant seeds.

Globe artichoke. Although primarily a vegetable, the artichoke produces most attractive silver-grey foliage from late spring through the summer. Its flower heads, resembling giant thistles, can be dried easily.

Achillea. This has flat heads of yellow flowers similar to yarrow. As soon as the flower shows full colour rub off all the leaves, dust the heads in borax and place them straight away in air-tight boxes to dry.

Hydrangea. Some varieties are much better than others for drying, but all will serve a purpose and provide a wide range of colours: pinks, blues, greens, reds, white. The flowers must be picked at the right moment, when the petals have lost their first softness and are becoming papery. There are three ways of drying: hanging upside down; arranging in water in a warm room; placing for a few weeks in a solution of glycerine and water.

Ferns and **bracken.** These are best placed between newspaper just as they are taking up colour and before they start to shrivel. Put the newspaper under the carpet for a few weeks, and generally the leaves will remain flat throughout the winter. If they start to curl put them back under the carpet.

Preserving your materials

Many types of foliage, such as beech, lime, oak and eucalyptus, can be preserved by means of a half-and-half solution of glycerine and warm water. Make up the solution in a tall, cylindrical container so that the stems will be well covered. Hammer the bases of the stems, and if the bark is very thick peel some off to show the white wood. Allow the stems to stand in the solution until the foliage shows a change of colour – usually after a few weeks. Be sure that the foliage is not too far advanced when starting, or it will drop off before the glycerine has been absorbed.

Flowers, on the other hand, are preserved by drying. It is important to choose the right moment, when the flowers are at the peak of their beauty and just short of maturity. If cut too soon they will shrivel during drying; if too late they may disintegrate. Cut in small quantities, remove all the foliage and proceed immediately to treat the flowers.

Sometimes precautionary action is advisable before drying. Some flowers become very brittle when dried – clematis for example – and to stop any petals dropping off you should place at the base of each a spot of clear nail varnish or good clear glue – it must be transparent and

Beech foliage being preserved
in glycerine and water;
flowers being air dried

Gluing prevents falling petals

not stain the delicate petals. A small brush is useful for applying the varnish or glue, and a toothpick can be used for placing spots of glue at the base of petals. In other cases stems may become brittle: you can prevent this trouble by carefully wiring the green stem to keep it straight while drying. Internal wiring is best because it cannot be seen.

The easiest and most popular method of drying is air drying. Basically you need an area where there is constant movement of fresh air but freedom from dust and strong light. A cupboard beside a central heating boiler is ideal.

Most flowers are dried with their heads hanging downwards to encourage straight stems; but such things as achillea and honesty will dry quite easily in an upright position. Tie the flowers into small bunches and hang them out on a line just like washing (space can be gained by hanging some bunches on coat hangers).

Another method of drying is in borax or sand, or both together. Borax on its own can be very quick and must be watched carefully: too long in borax will lead to the development of poor colour. Sand alone – it must be silver sand and very dry to start with – works slowly, taking 10–21 days. The weight of sand can be damaging to fragile flowers, so it is mainly used for the larger ones such as zinnias, marigolds and roses.

More often used is a mixture of both in the proportion of 2 parts of borax to one of sand by dry measurement.

Carry out the treatment in strong cardboard boxes or polythene bags, placing the mixture carefully all round the stems to be treated. They must not be touching each other; and keep to one kind of flower per box or bag. The flowers should rest in the boxes on pillows of cardboard so that the mixture can be evenly placed around the petals and the weight does not squash the flowers.

One way of drying is to stand the flowers upright and sprinkle the mixture round them, resting each flower in a collar of cardboard (completely fill the area inside the box).

An excellent drying agent for treating many of the more delicate flowers is silica gel. Place the short-stemmed cut flowers directly on a layer of the crystals, which can be laid in the base of a polythene bag, spacing them out so that they do not touch each other. Large flowers preserve best hung up in separate containers. Cover the lower petals first, placing the preservative between each petal so that contact is made all over – use an artist's brush to hold the petals apart. (Not more than four ounces of plant material should be used to each pound of silica gel.) Cover completely with preservative and seal tightly with Sellotape. Put the bag or container away where the contents will not be disturbed: most flowers take from two to eight days. Once they are dry, pour off the preservative carefully and slowly until each flower is uncovered. Blow or brush away any particles which may tend to stick in places – if any preservative does stick it will take up moisture as soon as the flowers are arranged. Store until required in a bag with just a few crystals in the bottom. It is important to keep everything free from dust. You can dry the silica gel crystals in a low oven so that they can be used over and over again.

Leaves can be preserved either under the carpet as described for ferns or by pressing with an iron set as for synthetic fabrics. Place each leaf between pieces of waxed paper, then coat the whole with sheets of newspaper. When you iron it the wax will melt leaving a protective coat on the leaf. Among the leaves suited to this treatment are caladium, hosta and maple.

It is also possible to 'skeletonize' leaves, though I never find it worthwhile, as you can get them from a florist. You have to boil them and then, at the correct moment, take them out and scrape them carefully to remove the pulpy tissue while at the same time leaving the vein pattern intact. After this drop them into a bleach solution for a couple of hours to get rid of the colour. Place between paper towels to dry, and then weight down to get them flat.

Berried subjects can be treated by brushing over with clear shellac and alcohol in equal proportions. This will be invisible when dry and will keep the berries intact for a long time. Hang upside down to dry. (It is better to do this job out of doors, where drips cannot do any damage, and safely away from fires or naked flames.) Bulrushes can be sprayed with hair lacquer to stop them splitting. Shellac can also be painted on to cones and branches both to preserve them and to give them a lustre.

Paint berries with shellac and alcohol

Containers

When you are making arrangements with dried flowers there is no need to worry about whether or not the container holds water. This is a great advantage, because it is still possible to pick up interesting old containers in antique shops and such places, and these often either have cracks or are so old that a lining would be necessary before they could hold water.

Indeed, anything attractive that will cover up the mechanics and hold the stems firmly can be used provided that it is in keeping with the flower arrangement. As a rule it is best to keep to simple and inexpensive containers, and in some instances no container is necessary at all – I am thinking of the garlands and walldrops one can make by fixing flowers and foliage to a background of material and hanging them on the wall. The following list covers enough to cater for all needs:

wood and basket work
metals – silver, copper, brass, pewter, tin, etc.
china and pottery
glass vases and bowls
small frames and glass domes
home-made containers

Various containers

Wooden containers are particularly suited to simple arrangements of mixed dried foliage, seed heads, wood roses and the yellow-brown flowers of helichrysum. They can take many forms: hollowed-out logs, carved bowls, an old tea caddy. We have at the Flower School a beautiful carved top from an old wooden column which has been hollowed out: this is quite excellent for a room with a lot of wood panelling.

Baskets of a good simple shape are always popular, and even the ordinary garden trug can look attractive filled for the winter with preserved flowers, grasses, seed heads and foliage. All manner of baskets are on sale in flower shops and garden centres today: another good source is any shop run by blind or handicapped people's associations.

All the metals are useful; but especially good are **copper** and **brass** with their warm colouring that develops over the years from constant cleaning. They will take all the soft browns, greens, yellows and straw colours extremely well. **Pewter** is excellent for the pinky-mauve colourings found in dried hydrangea, helipterum, statice etc. Try to sort out the materials into the right colour groups for each metal. **Silver** is perhaps a little too grand; but a pretty little cake basket or candlestick can be attractive filled with such things as rhodanthe, sea holly and sea lavender.

China and **pottery** offer plenty of scope, and a wide range of shapes is possible – always aiming at the rather heavy, chunky shapes for the bulky drieds, seed pods etc., and at pretty little delicate shapes for the smaller drieds – fairy flowers etc.

Perhaps coloured **glass** rather than plain, and crystal is better for dried flowers: being coloured it does not allow the mechanics to show and spoil the look of the arrangement. All shapes and sizes can be used, and of course you do not have to worry about watertightness.

Arrangements in small **frames** can be most attractive if very carefully made and in keeping with the size of the frame. To a suitable frame fit a background: hessian, velvet and heavy linen are all good and come in excellent colours. Arrange the flowers carefully into a pretty bunch or spray, either fixing them into a small block of Oasis or attaching them to the background itself. If the arrangement is to be covered by glass you will need a really deep frame. The frame, of course, can be of any colour; but gilt for a yellow-brown-green arrangement and silver for blues and pinks are the most satisfactory.

The Victorian **glass dome** is back in vogue again and can be most attractive. Fix a shaped piece of Styrofoam to the wooden base (covered with felt, velvet or some other suitable material of the required colour); then into this tuck all your seed heads, flowers and foliage in a mass of interesting colours and shapes. The dome will provide excellent protection from dust and accidental knocks. The addition of a pretty butterfly will gain that little extra touch of interest.

There are plenty of possibilities for **home-made** containers. A good, strong, upright tin cylinder (such as Bath Oliver biscuits come in) can be covered with a straw-coloured wallpaper or a suitable hessian. Or polish up the top surface of a large offcut of timber and affix a shallow tin lid containing Plasticine or Oasis: the tin will not show when the flowers are arranged in it and the effect is most pleasing. Or cover the bottom half of an old wine bottle with plaited raffia or string and arrange it simply with a branch of beech treated with glycerine.

Mechanics

If flowers and foliages, whether dried or fresh, are to be part of the overall decoration of a room, the first essential of successful arranging may be said to be the mechanics of the job – that is to say, the various means by which flowers can be made to remain in the exact position required. Once you have mastered the simple mechanics you will find that you can work easily and quickly with real pleasure and have the satisfaction of making a really attractive flower arrangement.

Ordinary **wire netting** is the most generally useful of all flower supporters. It should be of fairly large mesh and made from pliable wire. It is a mistake to use the small-mesh netting: when crumpled up it will only allow very thin stems to pass through it and many dried stems, although thinner than when in a fresh state, still remain quite thick. The netting can be used in two ways. One is to cut it into a square or rectangle and then fold or crumple it up into an open-work tangle. The amount used will depend on the size of the vase. Ideally, the stems should pass through three or four layers: this will give adequate support. For a shallow vase two or three layers are quite sufficient. The bottom layer should be on the base of the container when the vase is completed. The other way to use wire netting is to combine it with a block of **Oasis**, just placing it as a layer over the block to help hold it together: the stems pass through the netting and are held firm by the Oasis. If extra support is needed with either method to hold a difficult stem, cut a strand of the wire netting and pull it up carefully wrapping it round the offending stem. This need not show when the arrangement is completed.

When you are using a shallow bowl, it may be necessary to secure the netting to stop it rocking. This can be easily achieved by pulling some of the netting outwards to form small 'ears' which are pinched over the rim of the vase. Another method is to tie the netting with string or raffia just as you would tie a parcel, or with Oasis tape, just catching it round the netting in three or four places.

Arrangement in progress

When using wire netting in a glass vase, you will want to secure it in such a way as not to show when the flowers are arranged. Make a tangle of netting to fill the top third of the vase and hook it carefully over the rim of the glass. Make use of downward curving stems and leaves over the edge of the vase to conceal the netting.

The **pin-holder**, which originated in Japan, is not a great amount of use with thin-stemmed dried materials, but it has found a new function as an Oasis-holder, in the form of a heavy base with a few pins on which the Oasis is impaled. Oasis used in a dry form for dried flowers is light and does tend to fall over unless weighted in some way, and the pin-holder is ideal for this. Again, if Oasis is not to be used, a little ball of wire netting can be impaled on a pin-holder, and thin stems will then be quite firmly secured.

There is now on the market a form of Oasis which is very hard, so that all stems have to be mounted on wires which can then be pressed into the Oasis. It is useful for making flower balls and cones because it does not fall to pieces as the spongy type so easily does.

Finally, other materials can be used for holding dried materials, such as **sand** or **gravel**; but these are not easy to use and the advantage of their weight is easily offset by their many disadvantages such as being messy to use and damaging to some containers.

Eight
arrangements

POT-POURRI (previous page)

This elaborate mélange of foliages, flowers and seed heads, many of them to be found growing wild in the hedgerow, will keep autumn's memory alive the winter through.

The container is a very old copper bowl into which a small block of Oasis is fixed with a little wire netting. The individual components are: branches of beech and lime treated with glycerine; tall, upstanding bulrushes to emphasize the centre; spiky teazle heads; the yellow, flat-headed flowers of achillea; South African wood roses; and seed heads of poppy, lily and the South African leucodendron (alder cones would do as well).

The outline was sketched first with the bulrushes and foliage, then filled in with the other materials, the density increasing towards the hub of the arrangement. This kind of shape is designed to be viewed from the front, but it is still important to give it some depth by letting some of the flowers and seed heads project forward.

HANGING LANTERNS

Branches of physalis, also called Chinese lantern, festoon a hanging container in the form of a birdcage. A little weight is added to the centre of the arrangement by hydrangea flowers.

Care has been taken not to obscure the container while still being generous with materials — important when it is of an original or unusual nature like this one.

UNDER GLASS

Here an old Victorian glass dome covers a wide variety of materials in a small space: xeranthemum, rhodanthe, nigella, acroclinium, fairy flowers and catananche buds. The delicate silvery membranes from honesty seed pods give an idea of the small scale of the arrangement, which of course is designed for all-round viewing.

The great virtue of the dome is that it will keep the flowers clean and dry indefinitely: such an arrangement will last for many years.

HORN OF PLENTY

This generous display is economically created from stems of moluccella together with five zinnias. The container is a basket-work cornucopia, and a block of Oasis in the mouth of the horn holds the arrangement together.

Note how the arrangement picks up and extends the basic shape of the cornucopia: the zinnias state the line while moluccellas discreetly enlarge upon it and soften the outlines.

The moluccellas were air dried by hanging in a warm atmosphere; the zinnias were dried in a mixture of sand and silica gel. The basket was fixed to an oblong wooden base to make it stand.

CHRISTMAS HAMPER

A simple hamper basket with its lid propped open is here
filled to overflowing with hydrangeas and gaily coloured
statice (*sinuata*) — two easily dried and long-lasting flowers.
This is a case where the arrangement ignores the neutral
shape of the container and creates an asymmetrical form of
its own. The colour scheme is largely a disposition of
merging blocks rather than individually contrasted stems.
The stems are kept in position by being threaded through a
base of wire netting: statice stems often need thinning out to
achieve a satisfactory shape. Seed pods and foliage might
have been added to increase size and colour range; on the
other hand the outstanding characteristic of this arrangement
is its concentration, which could too easily be diffused.

GRASSES GALORE

A small bowl set in the upper of two offcuts of timber holds
this selection of ornamental grasses. The bark is left on the
wood for effect, but the offcuts could equally have been
stripped and polished. A few green hydrangea heads add
weight to the centre of the arrangement.

As with the hamper of statice and hydrangeas, the neutral
'container' leaves free choice of shape; but note how the
overlapping of the two pieces of timber is reflected in the
overall balance.

STILL LIFE

This collage is comprised of helichrysum, fairy flowers, a few grasses, some alder cones bleached and dried and sprays of lime treated with glycerine.

The frame is a small picture frame with a canvas background. The materials can be either arranged in a small block of Oasis or attached directly to the canvas.

It is important, of course, to see that the colouring of the frame matches the arrangement: the brown and gilt of this one corresponds very naturally to the colours of the materials. If a deeper frame is used the arrangement can be covered with glass, which of course will keep it clean and dry and prolong its life.